THE ANIMAL TOO BIG TO KILL

THE ANIMAL TOO BIG TO KILL

SHANE McCRAE

POEMS

WINNER OF THE LEXI RUDNITSKY EDITOR'S CHOICE AWARD

A KAREN & MICHAEL BRAZILLER BOOK
PERSEA BOOK / NEW YORK

Persea Books, Inc.
277 Broadway
New York, NY 10007

Library of Congress Cataloging-in-Publication Data

McCrae, Shane, 1975–
[Poems. Selections]
The animal too big to kill : poems / Shane McCrae. — First edition.
        pages   cm
"Winner of the Lexi Rudnitsky Editor's Choice Award."
"A Karen & Michael Braziller Book."
Includes bibliographical references.
ISBN 978-0-89255-464-5 (original trade pbk. : alk. paper)
I. Title.
PS3613.C385747A6 2015
811'.6—dc23
            2015026718

Designed by Rita Lascaro

Printed in the United States of America
First Edition

To Melissa, who frees

CONTENTS

Remember those who are in prison, as though
you were in prison with them; those who are being tortured,
as though you yourselves were being tortured.

—HEBREWS 13:3

MORNING PRAYER

With Every Gesture

I haven't Lord I haven't You I have-
n't praised enough You Lord although I with or would
With every poem praise You every   breath and eve-

ry gesture praise you Lord and many in the months
In the first months
After I Lord converted after I   / Lord reconciled myself with my conversion many days

I started by invoking You Your
name   / As I had learned to do in catechism
At the beginnings of my prayers

So that the day would be a prayer
And every gesture   I made in the day
Believing

I could stay / Cool   in the hot day
by running in the shadow of a cloud

The Animal Too Big to Kill

Lord I have eaten and I think I won't
anymore eat　　/ Animals
many times my weight / In animals

enough that were they resurrected and combined
Like the heroic robot　　in that cartoon I somehow always missed
And always looked　　forward to as a child

Lord they would be an animal / Finally too big to kill
Except by You who would
Shatter the sky and hurl the burning blue whale-sized shards down to do it

Lord even though You wouldn't have to break the sky to do it
And I accept I need to be reminded
I can't escape responsibility

for being the kind of creature that requires signs Lord from You
Merely by now refusing to participate
in the killing of some of the sometimes instruments through which Your signs / Pass

as they pass through every creature　　Lord and every object You I know

Killing the animal too big to kill would be a sign
And I accept I can't escape being grateful for Your signs

Being the kind of creature
that requires Your signs   / Because You Lord have made me wondrous
Beginning with my always I imagine it to be

an ugly mush but really it's
I think I've read   / Harder than that
brain and the thinking it might someday do

Because Lord I might someday think
Until that day and after   I require signs / Lord and I can't escape
being grateful for Your signs

Because my body not my brain responds to them   and You I know
Killing the animal too big to kill would be a sign
Lord as I took it for a sign

When fifteen years ago I prayed to be convinced
and drove to the monastery in Mount Angel and
Two tall firs

across from each other on either side of the narrow road to the monastery

Were struck by lightning

rare Oregon lightning on a barely misting afternoon

And fell across the road and Lord I couldn't leave

I took it for a sign   and I believed

And that was when   the moment when   I understand the language now

The moment I was born again

The moment I believed I

Had seen God kill for me

Lord was the moment I became a human being

As You I know

killing the animal too big to kill would be a sign

On the First Day of the Last Week of His Life
Jesus Overturns the Tables of the Money-Changers

I wrote to a friend   yesterday and told him my new poems were
About or I was trying to say
Something about   money to God

I think   and I don't understand it why I think it Lord You don't
Understand money
but of course You do   / And maybe even

Lord if You were You You   on Earth used money maybe You
Didn't just overturn the tables of the money-changers
Maybe You sometimes ached to not

Lord have enough for even a few figs   / Maybe You hated figs and always had or always the
Conditioned always of a life here
hated figs   / And maybe figs were usually

The cheapest food available and still You sometimes didn't have enough
Maybe You suffered in Your body first the suffering of in Your body Lord
Inhabiting Your poverty

Maybe Your body Lord was shaped by foods You hated
Maybe You sometimes walking to the market / Felt everybody even only
for a moment   / Glancing at You

knew Lord You lived on figs

Lord and You hated figs and always had

And on the day You overturned the tables of the money-changers

You also cursed   a fig tree never to produce   / Fruit again

because You had come to it hungry Lord

and found it barren

Mary Massages His Feet with Perfume Worth
What a Worker Makes in a Year

I would have Lord   as Judas did   wondered and maybe if
I had been brave   as Judas was
I might have said   / Something about it why the

Perfume Mary massaged Your feet with wasn't / Instead
sold and the money given to the poor
A few years back I worked Lord   in a factory making

parts for truck   / Engines I think   I wasn't sure then and I'm not sure now
I didn't mind the work   except the standing hurt my feet
It got so bad eventually I had to quit

I was a temp   anyway and I didn't   care what the boss thought / I didn't
know who the boss *was* but
I didn't want to disappoint the agency

still   / Eventually it got so bad I had to quit
But at the last station I worked   for the first time I got to sit
Nobody told me Lord I could

Nobody told me Lord I couldn't I just grabbed a stool and sat
Like anything I made there Lord I couldn't tell You now what
The name of the thing I made there was

But sparks flew from the machine and burned my forearms
past my gloves   / And Lord   I didn't mind the sparks I got to sit
I got to sit   Lord at that station for I think

a good ten minutes   / Before a worker I had never met
Threw her gloves down and walked from her
Station across the floor   / To tell me not to sit on my ass anymore

And then she walked off somewhere disappeared in the pallet stacks
I hadn't said   anything back   / Or honestly I might have said *Okay*
Not drawn out   quick and scared

She was the only woman I ever saw
close to my age on the floor
After she disappeared   / A man who worked at her station at

her table slithered   over asked me   / What she had said
and said she was a bitch   and told me not to worry
But after that I didn't sit

That was the day I quit   / I tell You now I know it Lord it love is truly is
Stronger than hate
Only for those who can afford it

Exile from the Supremacy

1. In the Supremacy

Growing up black white trash Lord even now
I wasn't sure which
parts of whiteness I could claim

But feeling it the rush of it   being black half-
Black feeling sometimes almost
white the rush of it   / Not claiming but

Being claimed by
The Oak Ridge Boys or who
Was it   who did that album with the spaceship banjos on the cover

Felt Lord as natural as money natural as
money feels Lord when after weeks without
any Lord not   a single

Dollar you come   across a little
And for the hour you have it
Or maybe the whole day   / If you   lucky can make it last the day

You are yourself again

2. In Exile

Growing up black white trash
In Texas Round Rock Texas meant
Growing up middle class

Growing up raised by whites   growing up raised by *nigger* not
Knowing black people use that word at all
Until you're twelve

And live in California
Lord / Growing up not   able to talk
to anyone about your skin

And what it does to you and kids you know and strangers
Growing up loving *The*
Elephant Man   on HBO

but you can't look at him
Wishing your skin could somehow
suffocate you in your sleep

Growing up drawing swastikas on t-shirts
Growing up raised   / By whites and white
things you can't keep

Empathy Erases the Heart

1. Empathy Conditions the Mind

Growing up black white trash you grow up told
The Nazis lost   the war because

only because they   / Ran out of gas
You grow up reading Sgt. Rock

comics years   later you remember   / Especially the one
In which Rock and his men

hide in a basement with a dozen Jewish orphans
and a nun   / Especially the pictures

Especially the faces of the children how
Fear was the only emotion

you could recognize in drawings the
one in which Rock

Offers a boy some chocolate the word / *Chocolate*
squeezed into a dialogue bubble

so narrow it   / Had to be broken in two places *choc*
-*o*-   / *late* and you couldn't read it years

Later you tell the story like it was funny how
You couldn't read

   2. That the Powerful Inspire Empathy in the Powerless
Growing up black white trash you read
Poetry yes   Shel Silverstein
Novels for kids about smart kids who don't fit in
And catalogues of war machinery

From mostly World War II and mostly
Lord   / You memorize the top
speeds and the maximum   payloads of Allied aircraft
Because the Allies won and Lord   / Because you grow up

raised by proud / Austrians you draw
Swastikas everywhere Lord / And you believe
somebody said it on TV   blacks
had it easier / In Germany   than in the U.S. in the 30s and

You want to live there then   to not be
Hated by whites   to kill with them

The Mountain Will Be as a Cottonwood Seed
Taken by the Wind in the Winds of the Last Days

Silence the black of sound
Silence a nigger silence the
nigger of sound
Silence the nigger monks
Meditate in   / Silence the nigger fills the abbey in the trees
on the mountaintop of the mountain / Silence
the nigger in which in / The mind is fixed on God

Silence the nigger the
monks sweep the floor of the abbey the / Dirt into piles
the mountain   / Will be   as a cottonwood seed
taken by the wind in the winds of the last days   / The nigger
the monks sweeping sweep the floor against
Wind being the body of silence
like / How voices are the bodies of words

like how everything on Earth
Has a nigger of itself

In of Body

1. Seeing Myself

Growing up black white trash I stood or stand

Maybe in my   memories only stood

Beside my skin   watching it always watching more

Closely than anyone

Even though I like   anyniggerone

Was watched in stores / Followed in stores and sometimes sure I stole

And Lord I don't   and do You see this far

into my head remember   / Was I excited to get my first bike I don't remember

Lord but I was excited so excited   / And I remember it

To get that weird tan coat with 18 pockets / I put it   on and felt

Criminal I felt   freed

finally seeing myself as others saw me

2. The Audience

Growing up black white trash you grow up wondering you

are raised

Wondering what you did and when Lord wrong to

Deserve your skin   / You grow up wondering you / You
grow up standing Lord outside   yourself and sometimes it's not bad   / You ride
your in your body bike

but no   matter how hard you pedal how
Steep Lord the hill you dive down head down head first almost falling like you're falling down
You stand

Outside yourself stand still
Like how it seemed when you were younger   Lord like the world moved beneath
The wheels of the car and the car didn't move

Growing up raised by white
supremacists   / You grow up skinned / You make
a puppet of your skin

What It Takes to Get the
Attention of White Liberals

Growing up black white trash you grow up marched

Hands up the barrel of a pellet gun

Stuck in your back   / Lord

to the bottom of the hill around the corner from your house

By the white boy from the house

at the bottom of the hill around the corner from your house

In the middle of the day

You grow up desperate for that boy

to be your friend that boy   / He sees your desperation and he hates you for it you

embarrass him with his own beauty

Your desperation and your ugliness

what you and he have been   raised to see as your ugliness

embarrass him   / He marches you

Gun in your back from / Your house around the corner

to the gates of his gated

white paradise

to banish you   / To make you understand

the only way you're getting in is dead

How You Are Owned

1. Slavery Is Forever

Growing up black white trash you grow up

knowing there are / Two kinds of white in the world one black

the   / White like the crayon / You grow up calling *flesh*

That colors everything the color of imaginary peaches

and the white like every other white thing / Lord   and the black like what your skin is like the

Black like what bad guys wear

The black like what you're not and what you are

You grow up drawing characters you never color in

Except for when you color in their clothes

Eyes mouths and noses floating in   what should have been

Emptiness but   you grow up seeing

white skin

You grow up owned by whites

not / Your body but your senses

2. Aspirational Harm

Growing up black white trash you grow up bodiless

Or what's a body

Without its skin white skin an x-ray   all the way

Down to the white bones white inside

Black skin a void surrounding no inside

You grow up no inside

you grow up void surrounding

You grow up never sure   you see yourself   in mirrors

You grow up thinking what you see / Is only it might be

90%   / Accurate maybe less

So that   when you at 14 for the first

time break a bone / You   when the doctor shows you

The x-ray think it looks

more real than you are

In the middle of a black void Lord you see

a broken white bone glowing

Museum of Science and History

Growing up black white trash you grow up
the only and complete / Whale skeleton
In the local mammals wing

Of a museum of science and history in a land-locked state
You grow up Lord   bigger and smaller than you are and were
You grow up white

But not a white that counts it makes
People uncomfortable
who when they think of white think of linoleum

You grow up a display case   Lord in which
Two hares have been arranged to illustrate
The influence of environment on coloring

The one   / Brown as the dirt it dies in
the other so white it disappears behind the glare

MIDDAY PRAYER

Kokoy

I will Lord praise You now   for my friend Kokoy

Whom I was sure I just this morning saw / Walking unseeing toward me   on the slowly

Brightening sidewalk brightening after

a late autumn thaw   / The snow

Becoming what it always was

and never was and couldn't be   / Water   then vapor

where it fell as snow

Died yesterday in the Philippines

And as he walked the man who wasn't

Kokoy walked   / I saw he wasn't   couldn't be

the man I hoped he was   / And still he was   / And full

Of life and also his own life

I praise You for the man I didn't know

and for the man I didn't know I loved

Claiming Language

my face, your face
—Anne Sexton

I don't just don't well not Lord *just*
Like the phrase *my wife* don't
Although I like and love her mine
Melissa

Although I happily own many things as many as my
Money will let me own
Although I don't say *keep* and it's
as many as my / Creditors will let me keep

I don't like Lord *my partner* or *my lover* or *my* anything Lord meaning her
Although I say *my wife* and want her to
Be mine   and I want to be hers   / And want her to
Say I'm her husband / I want her to

say *my*
and Lord I want to be possessed
knowing I can't be / As she can be
possessed

knowing it's in the bones of the
language me possessing her
I want a different language   / Lord not
a claiming language   / I want a language

like the language   Lord
our bodies use to free each other

The Seven Last Words of Christ

6. Father, into your hands I commend my spirit

The dream he most
Dreams often dreams is
A dream in which
He doesn't know he's

Falling until
He wakes about
An inch or so
Above his bed

And then he crashes
Face first bouncing
Into his bed
He never in

The dream falls backward
As far as he
Can tell not ever
Not once not that

He can remember
Although it's hard

Sure to be sure
And if you asked him

He would admit
He wasn't sure
Although how would
The subject ever

Come up or maybe
It would it proba-
bly would

5. *I am thirsty*

          if you
Maybe if you

And he were sitting
Together stoned
Together or
You wouldn't have to

Be sitting you
Could be in any

Position and
Maybe together

Lying on
A bed together
Would make more sense
But by then you

And he would have
Already had
This conversa-
tion or a con-

versation like it
Equivalent
Loosely in-
timate the kind

Of conversation
New lovers have
Naked people
Together who have

No history to-
gether except
They have consumed
Each other talking

And it might be
You haven't met
The person you
Will fuck tonight

And for the next
Six years I won't
Record the con-
versation here

About the dream
He most he dreams
Most often dreams
And even if you

And he did have
That conversa-
tion really he
Probably wouldn't

Talk about it
How he isn't
Sure whether he
Falls forward or

Backward because the
Dream always ends with
Him waking just
Before he crash-

es into his
Bed and he can't
Ever and hasn't
Once remembered

Remember an-
ything that happens
In the dream before he
Wakes in and from

The dream and he
Wakes like any-
body bleary
But not the same

Bleary he and
Anybody
Usually wakes in
Because he also

Wakes terrified but
It's hard to know
Sure why for sure
Because he can't re-

member the dream
Itself not ever
But only wak-
ing in and from the

Dream which might not
Be part of the dream but
A consequence
Of the dream and he's

Sure not sure whether
Consequences
Are parts of old things
Or new and sepa-

rate things their own
Things and so he
Might be in the dream
Assuming it's

The same dream every
Time the same
Which he does
That's an assumption

He makes because
It always ends the
Same way he might
Be falling back-

ward even though
He always crashes
Face first and it's
Sure also hard to

Be sure because he
Wakes terrified
Bleary ter-
rified which is

Repeatedly the
Worst kind of terri-
fied he has ever
Felt and may-

be that sounds strange to
You maybe if
You haven't felt it
Yourself you think

Bleary terror
Would be dulled terror
But it isn't
And if you asked

Him he would tell you
It's the worst kind of
Terror because
Waking bleary

Terrified feels for
A second the
Confusion dis-
orienta-

tion that first waking
Second like being
Lost in terror
Forever like how

It feels to be
A child and lost not
A small small child big
Enough to know what

It means to be
Lost or to have
Your mother die
And it's not just

Something you in
Your angriest moments
Which weirdly feel
In retrospect

Constant like you
Must have been angry
Every day
And most of the day

Every day
Even though you can't
Recall a single
Particular

Time you wished your
Mother were dead
To have your mother
Die and it's not

Just something you
Wished would hap-
pen but still small
That kind of lost

That feeling but
Only for
A second it's
Hard for him

Sure to be sure
Whether he falls
Forward or backward
In the dream because he

Wakes terrified and
Disorient-
ed in and from
The dream and he

Assumes he wakes
Disoriented
Because he wakes
Terrified but if

You asked him he would
Admit he might wake
Disoriented
Because he falls

Backward in the dream and
Wakes falling for-
ward so he could-
n't say for sure

Sure that he ac-
tually falls
Forward in the dream but
He crashes face first

Into his bed
And bounces and
How many times if
You really think

About it if
You really try to
Remember and
Then think about

It have you been
Terrified by
Anything
That bounces really

Which strictly speaking
He isn't not
When he wakes falling
Because he isn't

Terrified by
A bouncing thing
Because he isn't
Terrified by

Himself he's ter-
rified by some-
thing that was
Happening in

His dream and dreams
Aren't part of who or
What anybod-
y is not even

Their dreamers they
Happen inside
People as people
Live inside

Them and people
Don't live inside
Their own parts
But it's the oth-

er way around they
Just happen like
Your mother dying
Or it comes slowly

Like first she can't have
Sex ever again but
She doesn't say the
Word *sex* she says

Most of a sen-
tence leading up
To it and then
Makes a sound

That stops at her
Throat but includes
Her eyes because
The doctor screwed up

When he was sewing
Her back together
And then she can't
Control her blad-

der and you nev-
er see her clean
It but the car
Doesn't smell bad the

Next morning and
It must have been
Dozens of times but
Not even then you

Don't see it coming
Even then

1. *Father, forgive them; for they do not know what they are doing*

    and
Then her house starts
Filling with garbage

Because she can't
Clean it any-
more and you're
Too young to want

To but you're grown you're
Old enough you
Should want to but
You never had to

Before and you
Don't you just don't want
To you just *don't*
And now when you

Try to remem-
ber what her living
Room looked like you
Think it looked like a

Brain threw up in
It but you also
Think the remem-
bering itself

Feels like your brain
Throwing up
But you don't see
It coming then

Either and it's
A few more years
Before she dies
And by then you're

Mostly away
At school you were
The last to leave but
You left her too

What difference does
It make except
The last leaves knowing
Everybody

Else has gone
Already and
Everybody
Knew she was dy-

ing but you did-
n't know but whose
Life did she die
Away from out of

Leave   yours or eve-
rybody else's
Yours and eve-
rybody else

Knowing really
Just means you did-
n't know just like
Nobody knowing

Would really just
Mean you didn't
Know and you know
Now everything

That happens slowly
Eventually
Happens all
At once that's what

Dying is and
That's how his dream
The dream he most
Often most dreams

Especially
Happens and
Even though you know
It's nothingness or

It might not be
But even though
You know it is
You can't imagine

Being dead as any-
thing other than
Blackness not si-
lence not exactly

Because you don't
Hear anything
But it's the kind of
Not hearing any-

thing you hear
In your mind when
You don't hear any-
thing in your mind

When you just see
An image which
Isn't the same
Thing as silence

Because you can't
Hear them now
But you read somewhere
That in the quietest

Room in the world a
Room somewhere with
The most effective
Soundproofing people

Can hear their own
Organs working
And they can't stand it
Silence is for

Physical reasons
Outside the power
Of your imagi-
nation and when you

Try to imagine
Past the blackness
To nothingness
The blackness goes

Away but you
See letters black
Lower-case let-
ters on a white

Background jum-
bled as if they
Had been dumped out
Of a bag let-

ters and a few
Pink spots and a
Few orange spots
Just spots a few like

A cheetah's mixed
In with the jum-
bled letters but
Lots of white space

Between each letter
And every other
Letter but sometimes
The spots drift close to-

gether although
You don't see them
Move in your mind
But it's like you

Look away
In your mind you
Look at something
Else but there's

Nothing there
And when you look
Back the let-
ters and the spots

Have moved but could
You see it maybe
Nothingness
By not imagin-

ing anything you
Could glimpse it may-
be as it dis-
appeared imme-

diately the
Instant you stopped not
Imagining
Anything to

Look for it   disap-
pearing as you
Look your mind filling
Again with fear-

ful noise and is
It is it after
All blackness he
Remembers after

After he wakes
After he crashes
Into his bed
Since he doesn't

Remember the
Dream at all
Does he remember
Blackness and if

He does is blackness
The dream or is
The dream like where
Your mother is

And if you woke her
Would she remember
Where she had been if
Where she had been

Was nothingness how
Good would it have
To be

4. *My God, my God, why have you forsaken me*

to be there
In nothingness

How sweet you can't
Imagine it would
Be anything
Other than sweet

Like nectar not
From any real
Fruit but from an
Impossible

Ideal flower you've
Never eaten
A flower not
A whole one on-

ly petals rose
Petals or drunk
A flower's nec-
tar but you can't

Imagine the
Nectar would real-
ly taste as sweet as
You think it would how

Sweet would nothing-
ness have to be
For her to want to
Go back and you

Can't imagine
She wouldn't want
To go back even
With you right there

Whispering
Or shaking her don't
You always yes
You always do

Shake anybody
Sleeping too long
A few unnec-
essary shakes a

Few more for the dead
But you would too you
Would want to go
Back you don't

Want to die
But if you died you
Would want to go
Back if some-

body it wouldn't
Matter who brought
You back to life

7. *It is finished*

But she said no

Such thing your mother
Said no such thing
Nothing about
Death being a part of

Life she was just
Sleeping and then
She died and then
Something you had

Never seen before
Left her and you
Could see that it
Was gone and you

Look even now
And you can't see
It anywhere
And you had never

Seen it before
Before it was gone from
Your mother's face but
If nobody

Has it then every-
body is
Dead and if every-
body were

Dead you would know
Because you would
See that it was gone
From everybody's

Face and you don't
See anything
Anything you
Strain your eyes looking

Anything nothing
Is gone

3. *Woman, here is your son. Here is your mother*

       and when
Jesus dying
On the cross saw

His mother and the
Disciple he
Loved standing next
To her he said to

His mother *Woman*
Here is your son
Indicat-
ing the disciple

And then he said
To the disciple
Here is your mother
Indicat-

ing Mary a
Void where a body
Was when the body's
Still there you strain

Your eyes but you
Don't see it it's
Like nobody
Carries their own void

It's like a stranger's
Void whoever
Carries them all
Christece   consumed her

2. *Truly I tell you, today you will be with me in Paradise*

He closes his
Eyes to think
Harder about
The dream but sees

A wave inside
A small black box like
The kind the N
TSB uses

Like you would dig
One up and o-
pen it and find
The ocean inside

Living

EVENING PRAYERS

I Know It's Hard for You to
Believe You Still Benefit from Slavery

The boy in the picture is

Tied in the picture   to the post in the picture or

Look closer it's a pickaxe look

Away from his   / Face to the base of the post look

that's the head   / Of the pickaxe look

back to his face

He's not a boy his

face the expression on his face the sadness it

Looks like the kind of sadness usually / A grown man won't let anybody see

Usually if he has a choice / Now

look back to the pickaxe

back to the ropes

binding his wrists to the handle look his wrists

Aren't bound to the handle look they're bound

Together he's   lying on his side

Facing the camera curled

up like he's hugging his

Knees look   picture it   / He's lying in the dirt

The pickaxe handle

someone slid

Or maybe had to push

hard through the hole it   picture it

Hard through the gap between   the backs of his

Knees   and his arms   below the elbows   / The man is lying on his side

now   you

Have all the pieces picture it   he's facing you

not with his eyes but with his body the   / Convict if he   the black

man if he weren't   lying in the dirt his body

wrapped around the pickaxe the

Pickaxe would fall

The Calf

Lord I have eaten and I don't
Want to and have to
anyway / Sometimes because I can't afford to eat
According to my conscience animals

Lord many times my weight
in animals   in the past   / But since I started
eating animals again it hasn't been that much
I'm sure it hasn't been that much

Maybe if all the meat I've eaten since I started
eating animals again were piled and weighed
It would weigh as much as   maybe if my leg were cut off
Below the knee the calf   the shin   the foot

Were laid in a scale opposite the meat
Maybe the scales would balance

For the incidents that inform "On the First Day of the Last Week of His Life Jesus Overturns the Tables of the Money-Changers," see Mark 11:12-25. This poem is for John Gallaher.

For the incident, and the telling thereof, that informs "Mary Massages His Feet with Perfume Worth What a Worker Makes in a Year," see John 12:1-8.

The title "The Mountain Will Be as a Cottonwood Seed Taken by the Wind in the Winds of the Last Days" and the corresponding lines in the poem were suggested by the Qur'an, surah 70, ayah 9.

"Kokoy" is dedicated to Francisco "Kokoy" Guevara.

The seven last words of Christ are the seven statements Jesus made from the cross. In the New Revised Standard Version translation and in their traditional order, they are: 1. "Father, forgive them; for they do not know what they are doing."; 2. "Truly I tell you, today you will be with me in Paradise."; 3. "Woman, here is your son. Here is your mother."; 4. "My God, my God, why have you forsaken me?"; 5. "I am thirsty."; 6. "Father, into your hands I commend my spirit."; 7. "It is finished."

"I Know It's Hard for You to Believe You Still Benefit from Slavery" is based on a photograph by John L. Spivak. Also, see *Slavery by Another Name* by Douglas A. Blackmon.

ACKNOWLEDGMENTS

Thanks to Sarah Blake, Gabriel Fried, Derek Gromadzki, Melissa McCrae, and Heidi Lynn Staples for their advice and counsel. And thanks to the editors and staffs of the following journals, in which earlier versions of these poems first appeared:

Boston Review: "Claiming Language"

Divine Magnet: "How You Are Owned," "I Know It's Hard for You to Believe You Still Benefit from Slavery," and "What It Takes to Get the Attention of White Liberals"

The Journal: "The Audience" (as "Wondering You")

The Literary Review: "The Mountain Will Be as a Cottonwood Seed Taken by the Wind in the Winds of the Last Days," "Seeing Myself," and "That the Powerful Inspire Empathy in the Powerless"

MiPOesias: "Exile from the Supremacy"

Petri Press: "Kokoy"

PLUME: "The Calf"

The Seattle Review: "The Seven Last Words of Christ"

Verse Wisconsin: "Museum of Science and History"

West Branch: "The Animal Too Big to Kill," "Mary Massages His Feet with Perfume Worth What a Worker Makes in a Year," and "On the First Day of the Last Week of His Life Jesus Overturns the Tables of the Money-Changers"

Thanks also to the National Endowment for the Arts for its support.

The Lexi Rudnitsky Editor's Choice Award is given annually to a poetry collection by a writer who has published at least once previous book of poems. Along with the Lexi Rudnitsky First Book Prize in Poetry, it is a collaboration of Persea Books and the Lexi Rudnitsky Poetry Project. Entry guidelines for both awards are available on Persea's website (www.perseabooks.com).

Lexi Rudnitsky (1972–2005) grew up outside of Boston, and studied at Brown University and Columbia University. Her own poems exhibit both a playful love of language and a fierce conscience. Her writing appeared in *The Antioch Review, Columbia: A Journal of Literature and Art, The Nation, The New Yorker, The Paris Review, Pequod,* and *The Western Humanities Review.* In 2004, she won the Milton Kessler Memorial Prize for Poetry from *Harpur Palate.*

Lexi died suddenly in 2005, just months after the birth of her first child and the acceptance for publication of her first book of poems, *A Doorless Knocking into Night* (Mid-List Press, 2006). The Lexi Rudnitsky book prizes were created to memorialize her by promoting the type of poet and poetry in which she so spiritedly believed.

PREVIOUS WINNERS OF THE
LEXI RUDNITSKY EDITOR'S CHOICE AWARD:

2014 Caki Wilkinson, *The Wynona Stone Poems*
2013 Michael White, *Vermeer in Hell*
2012 Mitchell L. H. Douglas, *blak al-febet*
2011 Amy Newman, *Dear Editor*